NEW TECHNOLOGY

transportation technology

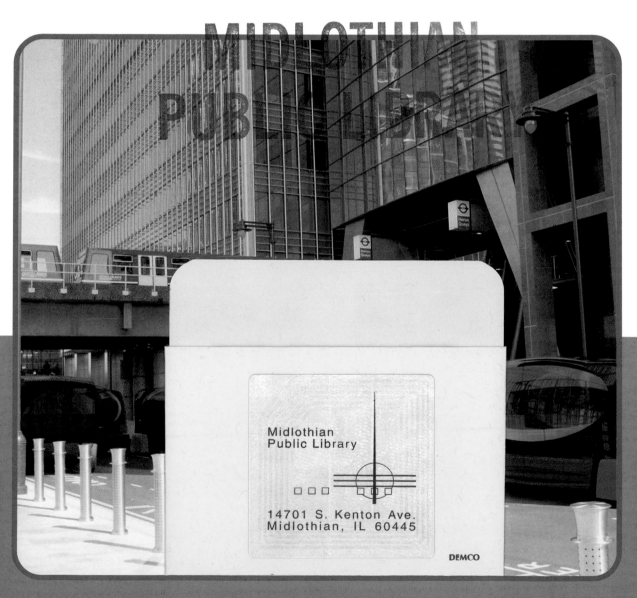

Brian Williams

A+

Smart Apple Media

Published in the United States by Smart Apple Media, an imprint of Black Rabbit Books
P.O. Box 3263, Mankato, Minnesota 56002

Printed in China

Library of Congress Cataloging-in-Publication Data

Williams, Brian, 1943–
    Transportation technology / Brian Williams.
        p. cm.—(Smart Apple Media. New technology)
        Summary: "Describes new technologies that are helping make road transportation, railroads, ships, airplanes, and space travel more efficient and discusses how transportation will change in the future"—Provided by publisher.
        Includes bibliographical references and index.
    ISBN 978-1-59920-166-5
    1. Transportation engineering—Juvenile literature. 2. Motor vehicles—Juvenile literature. 3. Transportation—Juvenile literature. I. Title.
TA1149.W555 2009
629.04—dc22
                          2008000442

Credits

Series Editor: Paul Humphrey
Editor: Gianna Williams
Designer: Keith Williams
Production: Jenny Mulvanny
Picture researchers: Rachel Tisdale and Laura Embriaco
Consultant: Dr. Charles Tennant BSc (Hons), MSc, EngD, ILTM, CEng FIMechE, Associate Professor, Warwick Manufacturing Group at the University of Warwick

Acknowledgements

Title page and p.21: Capoco Design; p.7 Diego Azubel/EPA/Corbis; p.9 James A. Sugar/National Geographic/Getty Images; p.10 Owen Franken/Corbis; p.11 Toyota; p.13 Dane Andrew/ZUMA/Corbis; p.14 NREL; p.15 Reuters/Corbis; p.16 ZAP; p.17 Toyota; p.18 Siemens; p.20 Siemens; p.22 Segway Photos; p.23 Advanced Transport Systems Ltd; p.24 Toru Hanai/Reuters/Corbis; p.25 General Electric; p.26 Kevin Lee/Getty Images; p.27 Mika Grondahl/Popular Science; p.28 Americanflaghip.com; p.29 foxxaero.homestead.com; p.30 Wallenius Wilhelmsen Logistics; p.31 Bremen Beluga Group; p.32 Airbus; p.33 Corbis Sygma; p.34 Lawrence Livermore Laboratory; p.35 Derimais Lionel/Corbis Sygma; p.36 U.S. Navy; p.37 Millennium Jet, Inc./NASA; pp.38 and 39 Lockheed Martin; p.39 bottom Anatoly Zak; p.40 NASA/MSFC; p.41 NASA; p.42 Norsk Hydro ASA

contents

introduction 6

CHAPTER 1 **road** transportation 8

CHAPTER 2 **railroads** 24

CHAPTER 3 **all at sea:** ships and ACVs 28

CHAPTER 4 **air** travel 32

CHAPTER 5 **space** 38

CHAPTER 6 **the shape** of things to come 42

glossary 44

more information 45

index 46

introduction

Most people travel every day—going to work or school, for example. New technology has helped people move farther and faster ever since the invention of the wheel about 5,000 years ago. In the twenty-first century, people travel more than ever before. Much of this movement is by road, and in many countries the fastest area of growth is in private cars.

There are now more than one billion car drivers in the world. Yet in many cities, cars and buses go no faster than horses and carts did 150 years ago. Private transportation (chiefly cars) now moves far more people on land than public transportation: buses, trams, and trains. More cars means increased congestion, more pollution, and more fuel used up.

Fuel Since the invention of the car in the 1880s, oil has been the world's key fuel. Current use is about 82 million barrels (1 barrel = 42 gallons/159 liters) a year. World oil reserves are estimated at about 1,000,000,000,000 barrels, though this figure includes oil deposits that are hard to reach. At present usage, experts agree the world will start

Number of vehicles in the United States 1965 to present

	1965	1985	2005
Aircraft	95,000	210,000	220,000
Passenger cars	75,000,000	128,000,000	136,000,000
Motorcycles	1,382,000	5,444,000	6,200,000
Buses	314,000	593,000	795,000
Trucks (heavy)	787,000	1,403,000	2,010,000
Class 1 (mainline) rail trains	27,800	22,500	22,015
Ships (over 1000 tons)	2,391	748	579
Recreational boats	4,138,000	9,589,000	12,781,000

Source: US Bureau of Transportation/Britannica World Data

This chart shows how the number of vehicles in the United States has risen. Only the number of oceangoing ships and mainline rail trains has gone down.

to run out of oil in the mid-2000s. It will certainly become more expensive.

New technology, using new fuels, can keep people on the move. Later this century, electric cars will drive themselves on electronic highways, while giant ships cruise the oceans. Trains will zip beneath the sea in tubes,

Morning rush hour in Beijing, China's capital city. Car use in China is growing so rapidly that congestion and pollution are major concerns in the world's most populous nation and fastest-growing economy.

and robot-driver buses will take people to work. In space, astronauts will build a base on the Moon.

How people in a sample of European countries travel (%)

	Car	Bus	Rail	Tram
United Kingdom	87	6	6	1
Netherlands	84	7	8	1
Hungary	60	24	13	3
France	85	5	9	1
Germany	85	7	7	1

Source http://ec/europa.eu/dgs/energy_transport/figures - 2004 data

This chart shows how most Europeans travel by car rather than by bus, rail, or tram. The same is true in the United States.

CHAPTER 1

road transportation

Every week, most drivers fill up their cars with gasoline or diesel. These fuels come from petroleum oil. The world is running out of fossil fuels, such as petroleum, gas, and coal. But fuel isn't the only problem. Transportation also damages the environment. It can be dirty, noisy, and dangerous.

Traffic-congested cities, such as Los Angeles and Mexico City, already have serious air pollution problems. As people get richer, in countries with fast-growing economies such as China and India, they want to buy cars. More cars mean more crowded streets, more ill health, and more pollution. Making cars smaller and lighter will help—bigger cars guzzle more gasoline. Traveling less helps too.

How can technology help?

Science can help by developing new vehicles powered by new fuels (such as biofuels and solar power) to replace fossil fuels. Computer systems can also help ease traffic congestion and make roads safer, cutting pollution, making the air cleaner, and protecting the environment and wildlife.

Limiting car use There are more than 6 billion people on Earth. If every one of them drove a car every day, most roads would be jammed solid. Around the world, cities have already begun to ration car use. Bogota (Colombia) was among the first; since 1983 it has had a ban on cars in selected areas on Sunday, so the streets are free for joggers, walkers, cyclists, and families with small children. San Francisco started a similar Saturday car-free

CHINA'S CAR USE

China is booming, and economic growth means more cars. Car ownership in Beijing will top 3 million in 2008. In the 1970s, 70 percent of Beijing's citizens used public transportation. Today, the figure is 24 percent. Yet journeys now take much longer. Traffic speed has slowed, from an average 28 mph (45 km/h) in 1994 to less than 8 mph (13 km/h) today. Beijing already has 400,000 deaths a year attributed to air pollution.

Lines of vehicles wait to pay at toll booths on the Bay Bridge. There are more cars in the United States than in any other country.

program on John F. Kennedy Drive, one of the city's busiest roads, in 2007.

Traffic management Technology can help keep traffic flowing. Congestion-charging in busy cities, for example, uses roadside scanners to "read" cars passing by. Similar scanning/charging systems will become a feature of many city roads and intercity highways. One of the first was in Singapore. Here cars are charged by electronic road-pricing between set times (7:30 am to 7:00 pm weekdays). On the windshield, the driver displays an Invehicle Unit (IU) containing a charge card, so he or she pays whenever the vehicle passes a platform situated at numerous points around the city center. The driver has a choice: pay and drive, drive another time, or use public transportation.

How do cars cause pollution?
Transportation accounts for around 13 percent of global warming, through the so-called greenhouse gases. This is a little less than farming, and much less than industry and power-generation, but still a problem. As a car engine burns gasoline, it gives off chemicals—hydrocarbons, carbon monoxide, and

THE CAR IN THE U.S.

- 30 percent of the world's passenger cars are in the United States.

- Roughly 95 percent of American households own a car.

- More than 55 percent of American households have two or more cars.

- Motor vehicles in the U.S. burn 140 billion gallons (530 billion L) of gasoline a year.

Source: World Book Encyclopedia/Britannica World Data/Wikipedia

Pointing the way to the future? This street sign in Paris, France, shows drivers of electric vehicles where to plug in to recharge their batteries.

What are alternative fuels? As the world starts to run out of petroleum, sometime this century, transportation will switch to alternative fuels. There are several on the horizon. Alternative-fuel cars cause less pollution than gasoline cars, but at present cost more, because they are built in small quantities.

Alternative energy sources include:

• Natural gas (in the form of compressed natural gas or CNG)

• LPG (liquified petroleum gas, usually propane or butane)

• Methane, hydrogen, nitrogen gases

• Electricity (from batteries or fuel cells, or from sunlight)

• Biofuels, from plants or microalgae

nitrogen oxide—into the air. These chemicals are harmful to people and animals. Cars can be made cleaner. Car exhausts are already "scrubbed" by catalytic converters, which turn the harmful chemicals into water and carbon dioxide (CO_2). But too much CO_2 is bad for global warming. Gasoline cars will never be really "green and clean."

Cars of the future In many countries, 85 percent of journeys are by car. Opinion surveys show that most people still expect to be driving "cars" of some sort in 50 years' time. Tomorrow's cars will probably have wheels, but their engines will be different. Almost all cars today have internal combustion engines, burning oil. Tomorrow's cars will run on electricity or gas. Others will be hybrids, using more than one type of fuel for different speeds. Packed with electronics, the cars of the future are already starting to roll onto the roads.

The hybrid car The hybrid car has already arrived. It is more economical on fuel, because it has two engines. One engine burns gasoline, the other runs on an alternative-energy source such as biofuel, gas, or electricity. In 2005, 212,000 hybrids were sold in the United States compared with about 9,500 in 2000. In 2006, Toyota sold 33 percent more hybrids than in 2005. With rising fuel prices and increasing concern for the environment, it is expected that by 2013 hybrids will account for around 6 percent of all car sales.

As hybrid cars become more common, filling stations will change. Some hybrid cars run on methane gas, for example, but the snag currently is that not many filling stations sell methane. Cars can also run on hydrogen and nitrogen gas.

The Toyota Prius (1997) was one of the first, and most successful, hybrid cars. It can run on just its gasoline engine, or electric batteries, or use both at the same time.

HOW IT WORKS

Gasoline/electric hybrid cars are more efficient than gasoline-only cars, because they can store surplus energy from the gasoline engine and brakes in batteries. The batteries then drive the electric engine to cut fuel consumption and take over at low speeds (for example, in town). The hybrid car can also use solar cells to recharge the batteries when the car is not moving.

Hybrid cars use less fuel than all-gasoline cars. They switch off their engines when stopped, for example at traffic lights, to save fuel. Plug-in hybrids have large battery packs that can be charged overnight. A commuter could drive 12.5 miles (20 km) to work and back, using only the electric motor, then recharge the battery overnight. With the gasoline engine as backup, there's little risk of the car coming to a halt when the power pack runs out.

HOW IT WORKS

The fuel cell changes chemical energy into electrical energy. A common type of fuel cell uses hydrogen gas as a fuel and oxygen gas as an oxidizer (an oxidizer removes electrons, or charged particles, during a chemical reaction). The hydrogen and oxygen react in a solution of potassium hydroxide in water (this is called the electrolyte). During the reaction, electrons move between electrodes (electric terminals) inside the fuel cell, causing an electric current to flow. The current continues so long as hydrogen and oxygen continue to be added to the cell. A by-product of the process is water.

FOR AND AGAINST

For
- Hybrid cars produce less CO_2 (carbon dioxide), a greenhouse gas thought by scientists to contribute to global warming.
- Drivers benefit in some countries from lower road tax and exemption from congestion charges (London, England, for example).

Against
- Larger hybrid cars are probably not much more fuel efficient than gasoline cars.
- They cost about 20 percent more to buy, so not many people choose them.
- They still burn some gasoline.

In a fuel cell, hydrogen (on the left) reacts with oxygen (on the right) inside the electrolyte. The hydrogen splits into +ions and −electrons. The −electrons flow through the circuit as electric current and power the motor.

Electric circuit

Motor

Cathode catalyst

Anode catalyst

(Oxygen) from air

H H H

Fuel (Hydrogen)

(Water) exhaust

Polymer electrolyte membrane

So the "gas station" of the future will actually be a gas station.

Gas cars Future cars could run on two common gases: hydrogen and nitrogen. Liquid hydrogen can be made from water, using solar power. This is done in the BMW Clean Energy system, used to power the BMW 745h, a hybrid that has a dual hydrogen/gasoline engine. Running on hydrogen alone, it can reach 133 mph (214 km/h), and has a range of 185 mi (300 km). The gasoline tank boosts the range by 400 miles (640 km). To run systems such as air conditioning, the car relies on an independent fuel cell known as a polymer electrolyte membrane (PEM), which uses hydrogen from the car's gas tank.

Filling up with hydrogen at a new gas station in the U.S. Hydrogen is the most abundant element in the universe, and can be extracted from water. It could prove to be the fuel of the future.

Nitrogen can also be used in cars. It is an attractive possibility, since nitrogen is plentiful—it's the main component gas in air. The only emission from a nitrogen car is more nitrogen, so the car is pollution free. Two prototype nitrogen cars have been developed in the U.S., at the University of Washington (the LN2000) and the University of Northern Texas (the CoolN^2). Both use liquid nitrogen, stored at very low temperature. One problem is how to keep the freezing gas from icing up the pipes in the engine! One downside of the nitrogen car is that to make liquid nitrogen is an industrial process, requiring electrical power, possibly from fossil-fuel power plants. However, unwanted pollutant gases (such as CO_2) can be condensed and separated during the nitrogen-freezing process, and (in the future) injected into used-up gas and oil wells, to prevent further air pollution. Nitrogen cars could start to have an impact during the next 20 years.

Biofuels Biofuels are fuels made from plants, such as corn and soybeans (U.S.), flax and rapeseed (Europe), sugarcane (Brazil), and palm oil (Asia). Biofuels can also be made from tiny living organisms, called microalgae, or from methane (a gas that can be extracted from cow manure). Biofuels can be mixed with petroleum diesel, to make biodiesel, which can be burned in

FOR AND AGAINST

For
- Biofuels are biodegradable (absorbed back into the environment). Biodiesel degrades as quickly as sugar.
- Biofuels are renewable.

Against
- More biofuels could mean fewer food crops. American farmers are being urged to grow more biofuels, so the U.S. buys less Middle East oil. But if too many farmers switch to biofuels, more people in poorer countries could go hungry.

Fields of fuel; rapeseed can be grown to feed farm animals and also to provide oil for use as biofuel. Many farmers could grow fuel instead of food—but will there then be enough food to go around?

conventional diesel engines. Biofuel crops are already being grown by farmers around the world.

Solar cars Sunlight is free and renewable. It can be turned into electricity, using solar panels. Solar energy works for home heating, and it can drive cars too. Solar cars are electric cars with a built-in recharger. (They don't have to be plugged in to the main electricity supply.) As long ago as 1985, "solarmobiles" took part in the world's first race for solar-powered vehicles, in Switzerland. So why aren't the roads full of solar cars? One reason is that so far

Solar-powered cars race at Suzuka in Japan. A saucer shape is good for absorbing sunlight, to generate electricity for the cars' motors.

solar cars are too light and flimsy to be safe on busy roads. Solar panels (the kind seen on sun-heated buildings) are heavy. Some solar vehicles have folding solar panels which are set up when the vehicle is parked, to top off the power supply.

Astrolab, from French manufacturer Venturi, is the world's first commercial solar car (2008). Its 16-kw motor is powered by solar cells molded into the car's carbon-based body. It has a "sunless" range of 68 miles (110 km) and a top speed of 75 mph (120 km/h).

Electric cars All-electric cars have been around since the 1890s. They are clean and quiet. The two main types are battery-electric cars (power from

WHAT'S NEXT?

In sunny Santa Monica, California, drivers of electric cars can "top off" at a solar array of photovoltaic cells. The sunlight generates electricity in the cells to fuel the electric car chargers underneath. The filling station can handle seven cars at a time, and any leftover energy is wired into the City Hall. This could be the shape of things to come in many cities with enough sunny days in a year.

batteries) and hybrid-electrics (a conventional gasoline engine drives a generator to make electricity). Batteries have to be recharged, and manufacturers are trying several ways of doing this. For example, General Motors' EV1 uses "inductive charging" (the charging mechanism is outside the car) while Honda's EV+ uses a "conductive" system (the charging mechanism is built in, and the driver runs a plug from the car to an outlet).

Sporty electrics The Tesla is an electric sports car launched in 2007. It is faster than many gasoline cars and can

Electric cars can look sporty. The Zap-X electric car has a top speed of 155 mph (250 km/h), and can be recharged in only 10 minutes.

run for 250 miles (400 km) on a 4-hour charge. Powered by 6,831 lithium ion batteries, the Tesla (named after a famous scientist, Nikola Tesla) has a top speed of 130 mph (209 km/h), on just two gears. It has a carbon-fiber body, so it's very strong but light. It is expensive though: $100,000. The ZAP-X is even faster—155 mph (250 km/h), thanks in part to its lightweight aluminum body. This car has 4 electric motors and a range of 348 miles (560 km).

The biodegradable car Cars are the biggest items of garbage most people throw away. Old cars end up as scrap metal. As much as 85 percent of a car's weight—mostly metal—can be recycled. The rest, much of it plastic, ends up as waste. In the future, more of a car will be recycled.

The biodegradable car will be made from plant plastics. One of the first is the Toyota iUnit, a prototype one-person transport revealed in 2007. Two lithium-ion batteries give it a top speed of 25 mph (40 km/h). Made from fibers of kenaf and lignin (natural plant materials), the car looks more like a collapsible baby stroller. It has two driving positions, twin joysticks instead of a steering wheel, a "drive-by-wire"

The Toyota iUnit, launched in 2007, is one of the most innovative transportation concepts unveiled so far this century.

WHAT'S NEXT?

Future cars might be made of carbon nanotubes—tiny, thin tubes of carbon atoms. Carbon atoms "bond" very tightly. This makes nanotubes tougher than steel, but as bendy as plastic. In theory, a nanotube car could repair itself by moving carbon atoms around to patch up holes, dents, and scratches. At present, such cars are some years in the future.

control system, and proximity sensors to keep it well clear of other traffic. Because it weighs only 397 lbs (180 kg), it uses very little energy and when it's thrown away, most of it simply decomposes.

Safety first Today around one million people are killed in car accidents around the world every year. Rear-end collision "beepers" are already a sign of smarter safety systems to come. Volvo has introduced a laser scanner to prevent truck collisions by slowing the vehicle; fully automatic braking to a halt is just around the corner. Alert systems (computerized voices, for example) must help drivers, without confusing them. Citroen and Jaguar sell cars with vibrating seats to wake sleepy drivers, and the Audi Q7 uses a vibrating steering wheel to warn if the car starts to veer off the road. Researchers at Oxford University found that "multi-sensory" warning systems, like vibrating seatbelts, alert drivers faster than eyes- or ears-only systems.

Roads of tomorrow Road engineering has already made driving safer. Examples are "retro-reflective" paint for signs and road markings (containing tiny glass beads to reflect car headlights); "Fitch barriers" (barrels of sand that absorb the impact of a vehicle); and "tone bands" or "rumble strips" (that cause the wheels to make a warning humming noise if a driver strays toward the road's edge).

GPS satellite navigation will be developed even further, so every car's computer will pick up data from satellite traffic-watch networks, helping drivers avoid traffic jams or bad weather. GPS Satnav systems will not just follow routes but also locate any vehicle anywhere in the world. Drivers in some cities, such as San Francisco, can already

A "head-up" display screen warns a driver when the car is going too fast. New technology can make driving safer, as well as less stressful.

check the Internet for color-coded traffic congestion maps. Manufacturers such as BMW are developing "interactive car-communication." If one car meets a patch of ice or fog, it will beam out a radio warning to all other cars nearby.

Smart highways, smarter cars

Many roads of tomorrow will be automated electronic routes. This will involve a lot of engineering work, over the next 50 years, to install electronic guides in roads. On these roads, drivers will hand over control of the car to an onboard computer, and the car will drive itself along the electronic pathway, kept at a safe distance from other vehicles by sensors in the vehicle and in the road.

WHAT'S NEXT?

The car of tomorrow will recognize its owner by "biometrics"—voice-recognition or eye (iris) identification. The car will start only for the right person. Seats and controls will adjust automatically to each driver's body. The car will speak to its owner, using a synthesized voice. Experts expect these features to be standard in the next 30-40 years.

Four-wheel superdrive Today's cars are inefficient because a lot of the energy the engine creates is lost on its way through the car's transmission to the

This car-to-car communication system allows cars to exchange data on weather conditions. For example, if the car's sensors detect that the wipers are on (because of rain), a "slippery conditions warning" is passed to other vehicles in the vicinity.

wheels. By the time the engine's power gets to the wheels and moves the car forward, about 50 percent of the original power created is lost. By 2025, each car wheel will be powered by its own motor. These superwheels will have built-in steering, shock absorbers and brakes, and be able to pivot on their own. The "eCorner" superwheel system is being developed by Siemens. Superwheels will do away with today's car engine and transmission, and be much more efficient, translating 96 percent of the motor power into motion. New-style wheels will mean that tomorrow's cars will be able to park sideways. (Siemens already has a system called Park Mate that can measure a parking space.) With superwheel cars, there will be fewer moving parts, fewer breakdowns, and cheaper repair bills.

The sound tube

Noise pollution is worst around busy roads in cities. One solution is to roof over the road. This has been done

A cutaway diagram of the eCorner hi-tech wheel. Each wheel is powered by its own electric motor, with brakes and suspension built in.

WHAT'S NEXT?

Tire treads (the pattern on the rubber) are designed to grip the road in rain or dry weather. In places with freezing winters, many drivers change tires to drive on ice and snow. The Q tire changes itself when it's icy. Retractable studs are pushed out by air pressure, for extra grip on snow. When not needed, the studs retract into the tire.

1 Wheel rim
2 Hub motor
3 Electronic wedge brake
4 Suspension
5 Electronic steering

in Melbourne, Australia. The city's toll-expressway system includes a stretch of "sound tube" which reduces noise pollution close to high-density housing. The tube acts as insulation, to shut off the noise from people nearby. Sound tubing could become a feature of inner city roadbuilding in other countries too.

City transportation By 2012, Londoners could be riding on a driverless "pod bus" which follows magnets in the road. The bus navigates using a system called FROG—short for "free ranging on grid." A grid of magnets in the road guides the bus along its route, and controllers can follow its progress on an electronic roadmap.

London could see these caterpillar-like "pods" alongside the city's familiar double-decker red buses. Above the street is a train on one of the city's overground rail links, the Docklands Light Railway.

Passengers call the bus from a mobile phone and the bus can redirect itself to collect them from pick-up points along the route. A prototype robot bus is due in 2008, with a system up and running for the 2012 Olympics. Pods will be linked up to form trains.

Hybrid buses For fuel economy, the "pod bus" will have an electric/biofuel hybrid engine. Hybrid buses are already at work in cities around the world, for example in Seattle and New York City, Valencia (Spain), and Mexico City (Mexico). London began testing double-decker hybrid diesel/electric buses in 2007. The buses offer a 30 percent cut in pollutant gas emissions. In typical operation, a diesel/electric bus switches from its "hush mode" electric motor at low speed (below 15 mph or 24 km/h) to a diesel engine for faster speeds between stops.

Bamboo bikes Over the past 50 years, more people have used cars, and fewer people have walked or ridden bikes. Yet walking and cycling are sustainable (no fuel is burned), healthy, and beat congestion. Many cities encourage bikes through cycle lanes and pedestrian zones. An interesting alternative to the conventional bike (made of metal, plastic, or carbon fibers which are expensive and nonrenewable)

WHAT'S NEXT?

Power-walking aids could speed up trips to the store or school. Take the Segway, a "personal transportation device" unveiled in the early 2000s. It has two wheels driven by electric motors and computers and gyroscopes for balance. By leaning forward or backward, the rider makes the machine go faster or slower. The Segway tilts backward (to slow down) when nearing its top speed of 12 mph (20 km/h). It also slows or stops if it touches an obstacle. The Segway has had its problems, and not everyone believes it is the answer to getting around a city, but it's fun to try.

American police in the city of Baltimore go on patrol riding Segway walkers.

is the bamboo bike, invented by Brazilian engineer Flavio Deslandes. Bamboo grows rapidly. It is cheap and renewable. It is light, but as strong as steel in some situations.

People moving People movers, or Personal Rapid Transits (PRTs), are the next step from elevators, moving walkways, and escalators. They are ideal for moving people around airports and shopping centers. One of the first was the Never Stop Railway, built for the British Empire Exhibition at Wembley, London, in 1924. A total of 88 carriages ran on a circular track, using a screw-thread propulsion system, never stopping. Passengers stepped aboard a carriage as it slowed to walking pace.

A passenger prepares to board an ULTra car at London's Heathrow airport. ULTra is one of the first automated people-moving systems.

The Jacksonville Skyway system in Florida was completed in 2000. Carriages run in trains along a 2.5-mile (4-km) track. There are two newer systems: ULTra at Heathrow Airport, London, and one at Dubai, both starting in 2008. PRT systems could become common in cities, to help ease urban congestion alongside light railways, trams, monorails, robot buses, and electronic roadways.

HOW IT WORKS

The ULTra system is a bit like a theme park ride with small electric cars running along a guideway. On ULTra, passengers wait just a few seconds for the next car. Each car seats four people and travels at up to 25 mph (40 km/h).

CHAPTER 2
railroads

Railroads can carry more passengers and haul more freight than any other form of land transportation. They can match airplanes for fast travel times between city centers (planes have to drop off their passengers at airports, usually many miles from the city).

Trains cause less air pollution than cars and trucks. GPS tracking means controllers know the location of every locomotive and freight wagon. ECP (electronically controlled pneumatic) brakes help make train travel very safe.

Developments in hi-tech trains include new power sources, improved vehicle and control systems to allow for faster trains and more trains on existing tracks, and automated rapid-transit systems.

Will future trains go faster?
France, Japan, and Germany led the way in high-speed trains (HSTs). New HSTs won't be much faster than the French TGV, which set a world speed record of 320 mph (515 km/h) in 1990. Some HSTs use tilting rolling

A new Japanese N700 bullet train slows down as it enters Tokyo station. These are the first Japanese bullet trains able to tilt around curves without slowing down.

HOW IT WORKS

Building new track costs a lot of money. To carry more passengers on existing track, a railroad can operate longer trains. This is being done on London's Jubilee Line (Underground). Trains can run closer together, thanks to new electronic signal and control systems to ensure safety. On commuter lines, double-decker carriages double capacity, though this may mean raising the roof of tunnels built in the 1800s for steam trains.

stock, to take bends on old track at high speed; an example is the N700 Shinkansen in Japan, due to start running in 2009. It uses less energy than earlier HSTs, accelerates faster, and has improved aerodynamics for a more comfortable ride at up to 186 mph (300 km/h). Japanese-built Javelin

trains will run shuttle services into London on the new high-speed line for the 2012 Olympic Games. They will run at 140 mph (225 km/h). California plans a high speed line that will run services between San Francisco and Los Angeles in just under two hours.

Hybrid trains Most trains today are diesel-electric (diesel-burning engines drive electricity generators) or electric (the current comes from overhead wires or an electrified third rail). A hybrid locomotive runs on diesel, but converts energy from its brake system into additional energy for motion and for storage in electrical batteries. A pioneer hybrid loco, in 2002, was Green Goat, a Canadian switch engine that gets 85 percent of its energy from 336 two-volt batteries. It's clean too. It produces less than 20 percent of the gas emissions of other diesel locomotives.

General Electric's Evolution *is a U.S. hybrid diesel-electric locomotive. It converts energy released from its braking system into electricity, to boost its performance and reduce exhaust emissions.*

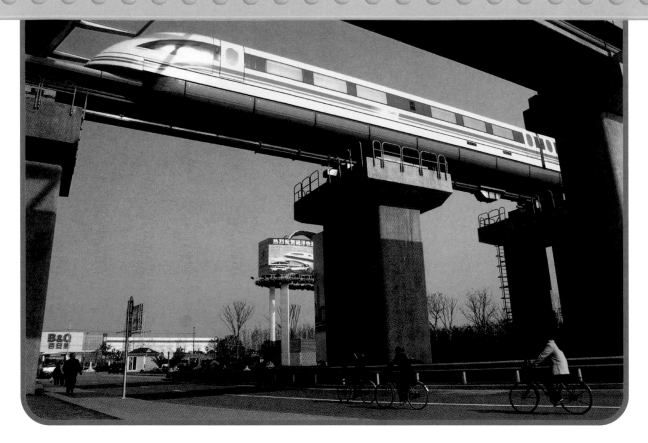

Cyclists pedal beneath one of Shanghai's maglev trains, which speed at up to 250 mph (400 km/h) along a 40-mile (65-km) track to and from the Chinese city's airport.

Maglev trains "Maglev" is short for magnetic levitation. Maglev trains "float" above a metal track, and are pushed along by a linear motor. Propellers or even jet engines could also be used to propel the train. With no wheels rubbing on rails, there is little friction so maglev trains are very fast. Experimental German and Japanese maglev trains have reached 342 mph (550 km/h). The first operational maglev railroad opened in Shanghai, China, in 2002. It runs out to the airport on 19 miles (30 km) of track at speeds of up to 311 mph (500 km/h).

FOR AND AGAINST

For
- Maglev trains are very fast.
- They cause little pollution.

Against
- They are expensive to build.
- Maglev trains generate from 62 to 90 decibels of noise, higher than most intercity trains. Compare that with trucks at around 65 decibels or jet aircraft at 105 decibels.
- The strong EDS magnetic field could affect passengers with electronic heart pacemakers, as well as computer drives and credit cards.

Rapid transit Underground trains are also the subject of new technology. New York City, along with other cities, plans to upgrade its subway system. By 2050, new trains will use Communication Based Train Control (CBTC). Transponders between the rails will link electronically with the trains, providing instant communication between each train unit and the control center. Trains will run faster, closer together, and more safely. In the future, rapid transit systems with individual cars that operate on their own will form trains and uncouple at stations to head off on another route. Standby cars will join trains automatically at peak times. Every seat might have a computer terminal so the passengers can work, play, watch a film, or just keep in touch.

This diagram shows how a vacuum-tube train will run through a tunnel anchored to the ocean floor.

WHAT'S NEXT?

Sucking air out of a tube (to make a vacuum) means there is no friction. A train running inside a vacuum tube could reach 1,864 mph (3,000 km/h). This is envisaged by two engineers, Ernst Frankel and Frank Davidson. In their futuristic design, the trains run through tunnels suspended up to 295 feet (90 m) deep in the Atlantic Ocean. By 2050, vacuum-tube trains could whiz from London to New York in two hours, faster than a plane today.

Maintenance shaft

Main tunnel section
Magnetic track

Magnetically levitated train

Emergency track

Anchor tether

Power supply

CHAPTER 3
all at sea: ships and ACVs

Ships are getting bigger all the time, especially cruise ships. *America World City*, a supergiant cruise liner (planned by World City Corporation, U.S.), will be one of three supergiant ocean liners: 275,500 tons (250,000 t) and 1,250 ft (380 m) long. It will carry 3,000 passengers and 1,500 crew. Future floating hotels could be as big as cities.

A proposed mega-giant U.S. vessel called *Freedom* will carry 50,000 people. More than 4,000 ft (1,220 m) long and 2.9 million tons (2.7 million t), it will be a motorized island, with its own marina, airstrip, and railway. Instead of a hull, 600 airtight cells will act as the foundations for the "city" on top.

Making containers go faster Most sea-freight is shipped inside box-like containers. Big ships carry more than 9,000 containers and usually take up to 25 days to journey between Europe and

HOW IT WORKS

The *ADX Pentamaran* will carry about 1,000 containers across the Atlantic Ocean at around 53 mph (85 km/h). Its ultra-thin hull will cut through the water, supported by four outriggers, like those on a catamaran.

An artist's illustration of the America World City, *the world's largest passenger ship, which will feature a planetarium, tennis courts, and a 2,000-seat theater.*

the United States. The *ADX Pentamaran*, a proposed hi-tech container express, will do the trip in three days. Designed by British engineer Nigel Gee, the ship will have jet engines to push it through the water faster than all but a few specialized vessels.

Wingships Wingships are vehicles that skim the waves. Hovercraft or "air-cushion vehicles" (ACVs) can travel over land or water. Wingships are bigger and faster, but can only move over water. They are also called "wing-in-ground-effect" (WIG) ships. They look like seaplanes about to take off, but never fly. Instead, they skim the water at over 298 mph (480 km/h).

The proposed Atlantis *wingship would represent a major engineering breakthrough. It would be 10 times bigger than any ground-effect vehicle so far built.*

HOW IT WORKS

As a plane lands, it seems to "float" in the air just before touching the runway. The plane seems to rest on a cushion of air, like an ACV. The cushion is produced by the plane's forward motion. A wingship makes use of this effect. It does not need air-blowing fans and a "skirt," like an ACV.

WHAT'S NEXT?

The biggest WIG so far was the *Caspian Sea Monster*. It was 433 ft (132 m) long and weighed 550 tons (500 t). A new type of wingship, *Atlantis*, would be ten times bigger: 5,500 tons (5,000 t). Designs show that it would carry 30 times the payload of a Boeing 747, and cross the sea at 466 mph (750 km/h), but it may never be built.

Do electric ships work? At least 13 navies, including the U.S. Navy, are planning all-electric ships. The electric ship uses a gas turbine, or a nuclear generator, to generate electricity for motors to turn a propeller. Another system uses propulsion pods. These are electric motors, each attached to a short propeller shaft, which is attached to the outside of the hull. Pods are lighter and easily serviced. Electric ships can also go backward as easily as forward—useful for docking in port.

Sail power Hi-tech sails make sense for big ships, as well as yachts. The *E/S Orcelle*, a 2005 cargo-ship design by the Wallenius Wilhemsen company of Scandinavia, will be a "green" ship: E/S means environmentally sound. *Orcelle* will use electric power, through variable speed propulsion pods, and also tap into wave power and the wind. It will use fuel cells to make electricity, and three rigid sails, which will catch the wind

SHIP POLLUTION

- Ships carry 75 percent of world trade, but produce less air pollution through greenhouse gases than cars.
- Ships use less than 3 percent of the fossil fuel we burn. However, most fuel burned by oil-burning ships is "bunker fuel," the dirtiest form of oil.

A model of Orcelle, *a revolutionary "zero-emission" ship. With its mix of power sources,* Orcelle *(named after a dolphin) will use only renewable energy, the first to do so since the big sailing ships of the nineteenth century. The funnel-like structures are rigid sails, covered in solar panels.*

and contain solar panels too. *Orcelle*'s underwater fins will convert wave energy into more power.

The kite-sail Ever been pulled along by a kite in a strong wind? The kite-sail, a concept from the German company SkySails, looks like a giant paraglider. It is flown above a ship and tugs the ship along, saving up to 50 percent on fuel for part of the voyage. The first ships with kite-sails took to the seas in 2007, beginning with the Bremen-based Beluga SkySails.

A ship being towed by a kite-sail. The sail is made of chambers filled with compressed air. It is tethered by steering lines to a cable. The cable can move along the side of the ship as the wind shifts direction.

FOR AND AGAINST

Wind-ships: could sails make a comeback?

For
- Fuel accounts for around 60 percent of the cost of running a big ship.
- Wind is free and clean. Ships could use kite-sails as extra propulsion units.

Against
- Wind power is unreliable. With no wind, a sailing ship stops. Most sailing ships are too small to carry much freight.

CHAPTER 4
air travel

More people fly every year. Airports get bigger and busier.
Airplanes burn a lot of fuel—thousands of gallons on each flight.
Jet engines contribute to global warming and air pollution through
carbon emissions.

At present rates of growth in air travel,
airplanes will use up all the planned
reductions in greenhouse gases in
other areas (such as factories, cars,
and houses) by 2050. Cars and planes
contribute to global warming through
carbon emissions. One survey, from
the Edinburgh Center for Carbon
Management, reports that three return
flights from London to New York—
20,816 mi (33,500 km)—emit 2,205 lbs
(1,000 kg) of carbon per person. That's
about the same as a year's driving in an
average car, around 2,425 lbs (1,100 kg)
of carbon.

Bigger jumbos The airline business
is dominated by two big companies:
Boeing (U.S.) and Airbus (Europe). The
Airbus A380 is a "super jumbo," which
carries 555 people. It is an updated
version of the classic jumbo jet. In
contrast, Boeing's hi-tech 787
Dreamliner, rolled out in 2007, seats
half as many people. But Boeing claims
its hi-tech design, using carbon fiber
instead of traditional metal-alloy,
makes the Dreamliner lighter and more
fuel efficient. It also means it can have
larger windows, giving passengers a
better view.

*Passengers try out the seats in the wide cabin of the Airbus A380, the world's newest and
biggest jumbo jet.*

WHAT'S NEXT?

The "flying wing" triangular shape for aircraft was first tried in the 1940s. It's now called a "blended wing body" (BWB). A flying wing flies well at high altitude. An experimental flying wing, the Boeing X-48B, could lead to the first commercial BWB airliner by 2020.

Why no new Concorde? Very fast fighter planes fly at Mach 3 (three times the speed of sound), but carry only one or two people. Most airliners (with up to 350 passengers) fly at just under Mach 1 (Mach 1 is the speed of sound). That's roughly 600 mph (965 km/h)—about half as fast as Concorde. Like all supersonic aircraft, Concorde made a sonic boom, caused by shock waves in the air. The noise meant Concorde was banned from flying supersonic across the U.S. This hit sales. Only 16 Concordes were sold to airlines.

NASA drew plans for a new High Speed Civil Transport (HSCT), a supersonic airliner quieter and cleaner than Concorde. It has not been built because so far engineers can't beat the sonic boom problem. So new airliners, like Boeing's proposed Sonic Cruiser, will still fly at Mach 0.98 (so no sonic boom). A plus for the Sonic Cruiser is its very long range: over 11,185 miles (18,000 km) nonstop.

Boeing's Sonic Cruiser will fly at almost the speed of sound. Were it to fly supersonic, it would produce sonic booms—noises clearly audible on the ground—and the plane would face objections from environmentalists.

Skipping around the Earth

HyperSoar is a design from Lawrence Livermore National Laboratory in the U.S. for a dart-like plane that will fly at Mach 10 or 6,700 mph (10,782 km/h). It will "skip" along the edge of the Earth's atmosphere, like a pebble across a pond. HyperSoar will climb to 130,000 feet (39,640 m), then turn off its engine to glide down. Its next engine "burn" will send it soaring back up again. And so on, until it comes down to land like a normal airplane.

Synthetic vision

In space planes like HyperSoar, passengers probably won't have windows. Instead, they will get a virtual view, with a synthetic vision system (SVS), already being introduced to help pilots and ground controllers. SVS provides a clear-screen image, even in fog. Like the simulated landscape in a computer game, it generates a three-dimensional color picture. As GPS satellite navigation tells the SVS system where it is, the virtual view changes all the time.

An artist's rendition of what HyperSoar will look like. It could be built in the next 10 to 15 years.

Return of the airship? In 1936, the hydrogen-filled German airship *Hindenburg* crashed in flames in America. This tragedy seemed to end the airship era. However, the airship could make a comeback. Airships are slow, flying at not much more than 100 mph (160 km/h). But they are good for lifting cargo. They can fly long distances and they give passengers a great view. Modern airships are safer, because their "lifting" gas is helium, which does not catch fire. Airships currently flying include helium and hot-air versions. The prototype of a very large cargo airship, the German *CargoLifter*, was flown in a small-sized version in 1999. If and when the full-scale airship is flown, it will be as big as the 1930s *Hindenburg*, and carry 176 tons (160 t) of freight over several thousand miles.

Inside a 1,081-foot-(360-m) long hangar near Berlin, Germany, engineers are working on a new generation of airships. The helium-filled CL160 CargoLifter is designed to carry a payload of 176 tons (160 t). The airship has eight engines: four for propulsion, and four for maneuvers while flying.

Electric airplanes Electric planes can be powered by current from fuel cells or sunlight (solar energy). The world's first fuel-cell powered airplane is the French DynAero *Lafayette*, an experimental propeller plane tested in the early 2000s. James Dunn, U.S. pioneer of the laptop computer in the 1980s, is one of the inventors hoping to build more electric aircraft, including one called "Electra-Plane."

Electric motors are quiet and clean, but electric planes are not likely to replace jets yet. They're too slow. But fuel cells could replace auxiliary power

The solar-powered airplane Helios, *photographed over Hawaii during its first test flight under solar power (2001).*

HOW IT WORKS

Solar-powered microlights could be the "air cars" of tomorrow. *Helios* is an experimental U.S. solar-powered plane, developed by NASA. It has already flown 18 miles (30 km) high without a pilot. It has 14 electric motors turning 14 propellers, and 62,000 fuel cells to collect sunlight. For the time being, it is just experimental, with no passenger flights in view. *Helios* is not much faster than a bicycle. It's too light and flimsy to carry passengers. But because it runs on sunlight, a solar plane could in theory stay in the air for weeks at a time.

units (APUs) in airliners. These units power a plane's electrical and air systems on the ground. Fuel cells could produce twice the power, for the same fuel cost.

Air scooters Personal fliers or air scooters look fun in sci-fi films. SoloTrek is a vertical takeoff and landing (VTOL) air scooter that can fly at 80 mph (128 km/h), hover like a helicopter, and has a range of over 100 miles (160 km). The idea is to produce

Solotrek is an XFV (Exo-Skeleton Flying Vehicle in NASA jargon). A joint NASA/Millennium Jet project, this one-person flying machine has two ducted fan engines and a top speed of around 62 mph (100 km/h).

an airplane that is cheap and easy to fly, to provide people with a bird's-eye-view whenever they want one—checking farm stock maybe, or surveying land.

Convertiplanes Airliners need long runways. Runways take up space, so most airports have to be built miles from city centers. Vertical/short takeoff and landing (V/STOL) planes could fly passengers from city center to city center. One solution is a "convertiplane:" half-helicopter, half-plane. The idea was tested in the 1950s by the British Fairey Rotadyne. It had a big rotor (like a helicopter) but wings with engines for forward flight. The U.S. Osprey tilt-rotor aircraft has the same V/STOL capability, tilting its rotor-propellers through 90 degrees to change from vertical to horizontal flight. It's a military plane, but a civilian version could operate in and out of city center airports—if it's not too noisy.

Gyrodynes The Groen Hawk 4 gyrodyne (2000) is a U.S. convertiplane. It can take off and land in less than 26 feet (8 m). It has a top speed of 149 mph (240 km/h). The U.S. Groen company has plans for larger convertiplanes, with rotors like the 1950s Rotadyne; these projects include the Gyrolifter transport and the Gyroliner commercial carrier.

CHAPTER 5
space

The U.S. space shuttles will be retired from space in 2010. A new generation of manned spacecraft will then take astronauts and tourists into space. The United States, Russia, China, Japan, and the European Space Agency are all building new spacecraft.

Orion *Orion* is the new U.S. manned spacecraft. *Orion* will fly to the International Space Station, and by 2020 will be ferrying astronauts to the Moon.

This artist's impression shows Orion *with the Lunar Lander in orbit above the moon. As in the Apollo missions, the Lunar Lander is the separate craft used to land on the Moon.*

HOW IT WORKS

Orion will be launched on top of the *Ares* rocket. Similar in shape to the 1960s Apollo spacecraft, *Orion* is three times bigger inside and packed with 21st century microelectronics. For moon flights, it will join up in space with a moon-landing module. *Orion* will carry six astronauts. *Orion* will reenter earth's atmosphere for a splashdown landing in the sea.

Ares: successor to Saturn

Ares 1 will launch *Orion*. The Ares rocket will lift a payload of 27.5 tons (25,000 kg) into Earth's orbit. *Ares 5* will be bigger, as big as the *Saturn 5* moon rocket of the 1960s, 360 feet (110 m) high. *Ares 5* will lift 140 tons (127,000 kg). These rockets will become operational between 2010 and 2020.

This is the version of Kliper *that is being developed with wings, but a wingless version may still be produced.*

The Ares 1 *launch vehicle will launch the new* Orion *manned spacecraft, which will replace America's space shuttle.*

WHAT'S NEXT?

Kliper ("Clipper") is a new Russian "lifting-body" spacecraft proposed for the 2020s. A lifting body is a wingless airplane. It is shaped like a cone cut in half. The shape gives it "lift" when flying like a plane in the atmosphere. Although simple to fly in space, lifting body craft are hard to fly in the air and land. So *Kliper* may be given stubby wings so it can glide down onto a runway like the Shuttle. If it ends up wingless, it will be landed by parachutes. The European Phoenix and U.S. X-33 are other lifting body spacecraft under development.

Space tourism In 2004, *SpaceshipOne* made the world's first privately-funded space flight: 62 mi (100 km) into space, though not into orbit. By 2009, *SpaceshipTwo* should be carrying space-tourists from Virgin Galactic's spaceport in New Mexico. A second spaceport is planned for Sweden. The folding-wing, two-pilot spacecraft will be lifted beneath a mother-plane, *White Knight Two*, then rocket away at 2,485 mph (4,000 km/h), to give 6 passengers a thrilling glimpse of space during a 2-hour trip.

Solar voyages Rocket motors burning chemical fuel (liquid hydrogen and liquid oxygen) are inefficient and slow, in space terms. Alternative propulsion systems for spacecraft include electric propulsion (using the sun's energy); the electricity is used to generate an ion-drive gas stream. The first ion-drive spacecraft was NASA's *Deep Space* probe (1998). For voyages to the edge of the solar system and beyond, solar sails could be the answer for the mid-2000s. There is no air or wind in space; a solar sail is "blown" by the solar wind, a stream of light particles (photons) moving out from the sun. A solar-sail spacecraft

A solar sail spacecraft, as it would look in orbit above the earth. The mirror-like sails are made of material up to 100 times thinner than a sheet of writing paper.

WHAT'S NEXT?

How about riding into space in a space elevator? The idea of an orbital tether, like a very long cable, reaching into space was suggested by Russian scientist Konstantin Tsiolkovsky at the beginning of the 20th century. It could happen by 2050. To make the tether, a rocket would carry the cable from a launch tower to a space station in orbit 149-199 mi (240-320 km) high. Space elevators would then travel up the tether, by maglev propulsion, and transfer passengers and freight to the space station, with no pollution, and cheaper than rocket launches.

would accelerate to 200,081 mph (322,000 km/h). It could sail to the edge of the solar system in 8 years, compared to the 40 years for the *Voyager 1* space probe, launched from Earth in 1979 and still outward bound.

NASA's proposed space elevator. Electromagnetic space vehicles will travel up and down the elevator, which will be geostationary. It will keep the same position relative to the ground as the Earth rotates.

CHAPTER 6
the shape of things to come

Transportation is a growth industry worldwide. There will be perhaps 10 billion people by 2050. More people will travel in and around cities, and unless air travel is restricted, more people will want to fly between countries. More goods will be shipped around the globe, by sea, rail, and road. This growth poses problems: cost, congestion, accidents, pollution, fuel shortage, and environmental damage.

Green transportation In the future, many people may choose to travel less—working at home more, by computer. But most surveys show that travel will keep on growing in the next 50 years. By then the world's reserves of fossil fuels will be practically used up. So before 2050, a new generation of vehicles will be in use, powered by alternative energies.

Public transportation will provide one answer to overcrowded roads. Public transportation was for many years underfunded, as people switched from buses and trains to private cars. That's starting to change. While some cities, like Curitiba in Brazil, have built integrated transportation systems, encouraging bus use over many years, others face severe transportation problems, caused by rapid growth.

Iceland, which already gets 72 percent of its energy from geothermal and hydroelectric power, could be the world's first hydrogen-based economy. By 2050, all the country's vehicles could be hydrogen-powered, like this bus.

WHAT'S NEXT?

By 2020, astronauts will be building a base on the moon. The base is likely to be built near one of the moon's poles, in the hope of using sunlight there for solar power and lunar ice as a water supply. The first missions to the moon will send robots to find landing sites, survey natural resources, and reduce possible risks in time for the arrival of the first astronauts. Four-person crews will then begin making seven-day visits to the moon until their power supplies, lunar vehicles, and living quarters are up and running.

In Mumbai (India), for instance, rail planners are replacing 8-car trains with 12-car trains, just to cope with the extra passengers.

Integrated transportation

Integrated transportation systems link up all the strands of a transportation system. Technology helps to keep travelers informed, so they can switch from car to bus to train to plane, and walk or cycle when they wish. Road-pricing and rationing systems (like the one in Singapore) will become more sophisticated. People will get used to paying to drive, just as they've gotten used to park-and-ride systems in towns.

The ideal integrated transportation system does not yet exist. In Genoa, (Italy), the transportation system already involves a mix of alternatives: controlled car access, two funicular railways, a metro (underground), hybrid and electric buses, a dial-up taxi service, and methane-fueled minibuses. London (England), will have new transportation links in place for the 2012 Olympics.

Traveling safely Technology must also protect travelers—by making vehicles safer and by improving security systems. Security has become a major issue, particularly at airports and train stations. Today security checks make air travel a time-consuming business. However, technology in this area is improving all the time, spurred on by international efforts to combat terrorism and prevent transportation crime.

Into the future By 2050, most cities will have a mix of transportation systems. There will be new shapes in the sky (like airships), on the water (like wingship freighters), and maybe underwater (like cargo-carrying nuclear submarines). This book has mentioned a few of the exciting possibilities. Some are already here; others are just over the horizon. Whatever happens, the twenty-first century will see a lot of changes to the way people get around.

glossary

ACV ACV stands for "air-cushion vehicle."

aerodynamics Study of the forces acting upon aircraft or other machines traveling through the air.

airship Floating powered aircraft, filled with a lighter-than-air gas such as helium.

biodegradable Able to be broken down by bacteria.

biofuel Any fuel made from plants.

biometrics Identification of a person by biological features, such as voice or eyes.

catamaran Water craft with twin hulls.

container ship Freight ship carrying cargoes packed inside large metal boxes that can also be carried on trucks.

diesel Heavy oil used in diesel engines (named after German engineer Rudolf Diesel, 1858–1913).

drive-by-wire Technology which replaces the traditional mechanical and hydraulic systems with electronic control systems.

ELV Stands for "expendable launch vehicle," a multistage rocket.

fossil fuels Oil, gas, and coal, formed millions of years ago in Earth's rocks.

fuel cell Chemical device for making electricity.

gas turbine Engine in which hot gases turn the blades of a turbine wheel at great speed.

GPS Stands for Global Positioning System, the global satellite navigation system.

greenhouse gases Gases such as carbon dioxide, ozone, methane, and nitrous oxide, believed to contribute to the greenhouse effect, or global warming, when they build up in the atmosphere.

ground effect Extra aerodynamic lift from a "cushion" of air trapped beneath a vehicle such as an ACV or wingship.

HST Stands for High-Speed Train.

hybrid Vehicle with two kinds of engine.

hydrocarbons Chemical compound of hydrogen and carbon, formed when fossil fuels are burned.

paraglider Flying machine like a box-shaped parachute, with air-filled wings.

payload The passengers, cargo, or bombs carried by an aircraft.

sonic boom A loud noise created by supersonic aircraft. Sonic booms sound like explosions and may exceed 200 decibels. Thunder is a natural type of sonic boom.

TGV Stands for Train à Grand Vitesse (High Speed Train, in French).

transponder An electronic device that picks up a signal and automatically responds to it. The magnetic labels on credit cards are examples of transponders.

more information

Books

Aircraft: Technology All Around Us series
by Kay and Andrew Woodward,
Franklin Watts, 2005.

Amazing Machines: Mighty Cars
by Ian Graham, Franklin Watts, 2006.

Travel and Tourism
by Carol Inskipp, Smart Apple Media, 2009.

Web Sites

Advanced Transportation Technology Institute
http://www.atti-info.org/
In-depth information about alternative fuels,
hydrogren vehicles, and more.

Argonne Transportation Technology R&D Center
http://www.transportation.anl.gov/
Read about the latest developments in
research on hybrid and electric cars.

How Stuff Works: Transportation Channel
*http://travel.howstuffworks.com/
transportation-channel.htm*
The articles and videos in the Transportation
section of HowStuffWorks detail the inner
workings of every kind of transportation
you can imagine.

Places to Visit

Smithsonian National Air and Space Museum
Washington, D.C.
http://www.nasm.si.edu/

National Museum of the USAF
Dayton, Ohio
http://www.nationalmuseum.af.mil/

Evergreen Aviation and Space Museum
McMinnville, Oregon
http://www.sprucegoose.org/

San Diego Air & Space Museum
San Diego, California
http://www.aerospacemuseum.org/

National Museum of American History transportation collection
Washington, D.C.
http://americanhistory.si.edu/onthemove/

Union Pacific Railroad Museum
Council Bluffs, Iowa
*http://www.uprr.com/aboutup/history/
museum/index.shtml*

California State Railroad Museum
Sacramento, California
http://www.csrmf.org/

Museum of the American Railroad
Dallas, Texas
http://www.dallasrailroadmuseum.org/

Gateway Colorado Automobile Museum
Gateway, Colorado
http://www.gatewayautomuseum.com/

National Automobile Museum
Reno, Nevada
http://www.automuseum.org/

index

Numbers in *italic* refer to illustrations.

ADX Pentamaran 28–29
air-scooters 37
Airbus A380 32, *32*
aircraft 6, 32–37
airships 35, *35*
America World City 28, *28*
Ares rocket 38, 39, *39*
Astrolab 15

bicycles 22
biodegradable cars 17, *17*
biofuel 8, 11, 14, 22
biometrics 19
Boeing 747-400 32
Boeing Dreamliner 32–33
buses 6, 21, 22
BWB aircraft 33

CargoLifter 35, *35*
cars 6, 7, *7*, 8–20
catalytic converters 10
CBTC systems 27
computers 18–19, 27
Concorde 33
congestion charging 9, 12
convertiplanes 37

DynAero Lafayette plane 36

electric vehicles 7, 11, 12, 15, 16–17, *16*, 22, 25, 30–31, *30*, 36–37, 40

FROG systems 21
fuel cells 12, *12*, 13, 30, 36, 37
fuel reserves 6, 8, 42

gas cars 11, 12, 13, *13*, 14
gasoline 8, 9, 10, 11, 12, 13
global warming 9, 10, 12, 32
GPS Satnav 18–19, 24, 34
Green Goat locomotive 25
gyrodynes 37

HSTs 24–25
hybrid vehicles 10, 11, *11*, 12, 22, 25, *25*
hydrogen power 12, 13, 42

integrated transportation systems 42–43

Jacksonville Skyway 23

kite-sails 31, *31*
Kliper 39, *39*

maglev propulsion 26, *26*, 41
moon 38, 39, 43
motorcycles 6
motorways 19

N700 trains *24*, 25
nanotube cars 17
NASA 33, 36, 37, 40, 41
nitrogen fuel 13, 14
nuclear power 30

oil 6, 9, 30
Orcelle 30–31, *30*
Orion 38–39, *38*
Osprey tilt-rotor 37

pollution 8, 13, 14, 21, 22, 24, 26, 30, 32, 41

Q tires 20

rail travel 6, 7, 24–27
roads 18, 19

safety systems 18–19, 43
sailing ships 31
Segway 22, *22*
ships 6, 7, 28–31
solar power 8, 11, 13, 15, *15*, 16, 31, 36, *36*, 40, *40*, 43
SoloTrek 37, *37*
Sonic Cruiser 33, *33*
sound tubing 21
space 7, 38–41, 43
space elevator 41
SpaceShipTwo 39
supersonic aircraft 33
SVS vision 34

traffic 6, 7, 8, 9, *9*, 18, 19
trucks 6

underground systems 25, 27

vacuum trains 27, *27*
VTOL 37, *37*

wave energy 31
wheels 20, *20*
White Knight Two 40
wingships (WIGs) 29, *29*

ZAP-X 16, *17*